EVERYDAY HISTORY

LIFE IN

VIKING TIMES

SARAH RIDLEY

W

FRANKLIN WATTS
LONDON•SYDNEY

This edition 2010

First published in 2007
by Franklin Watts

Copyright © Franklin Watts 2007

Franklin Watts
338 Euston Road
London NW1 3BH

Franklin Watts Australia
Level 17/207 Kent Street
Sydney, NSW 2000

A CIP catalogue record for this book is available from the British Library.

ISBN 978 0 7496 9612 2

Printed in Malaysia

Franklin Watts is a division of
Hachette Children's Books, an Hachette UK company.
www.hachette.co.uk

The text of this book is based on
Clues to the Past – Everyday Life in Viking Times
by Hazel Mary Martell
Copyright © Franklin Watts 1994

Picture credits:
Courtesy of the Trustees of the British Museum, London: 8.
British Museum, London/Werner Forman Archive: front cover tl & c, 6br.
C M Dixon Collection: 30.
L. Eilison/AAACollection: 7bl.
Werner Forman Archive: 7tl.
Michael Holford: 14, 26.
© Mats Wibe Lund: 10.
Ronald Sheridan/AAACollection: 22, 28.
© University Museum of National Antiquities, Oslo: front cover bl, 12t, 16.
University Museum of National Antiquities, Uppsala/Werner Forman Archive: 24.
Viking Ship Museum, Bygdoy/Werner Forman Archive: 20.
York Archaeological Trust: front cover tr & br, 4, 6t, 6bl, 7cr, 7br, 12b, 18.

CONTENTS

WHO WERE THE VIKINGS?

The Vikings lived over 1,000 years ago in the lands we now call Denmark, Norway and Sweden. They were mainly farmers and shipbuilders. However, their land was not very good for farming. Norway was very hilly, Sweden was covered in forests and Denmark had a lot of sandy heathland. This meant that when the population increased, there was not enough land for everyone.

So, by the end of the 8th century, some Vikings began to look for other ways to make a living. At first they raided towns and monasteries in other parts of north-west Europe. They stole the treasures and took some of the people back home to be slaves. Then they began to travel overseas to settle and trade, as well as to go raiding. When they settled, most Vikings farmed while some made beautiful objects from stone, wood and metal.

This stone cross was carved in the 10th century. It shows a Viking warrior with some of his weapons.

SOME IMPORTANT DATES IN VIKING HISTORY

793 The Viking age starts when Viking raiders attack Lindisfarne, off the north-east coast of England.

840 Viking traders from Sweden reach Istanbul, which they call Miklagard, meaning "great city".

874 Vikings from Norway begin to settle in Iceland.

886 England is divided and the Vikings settle in the part known as the Danelaw.

GREENLAND

Western settlement

Eastern settlement

NEWFOUNDLAND

ICELAND

FAROES

SHETLANDS

ORKNEYS

SCOTLAND

IRELAND

ENGLAND

DENMARK

NORWAY

SWEDEN

RUSSIA

Staraya Ladoga

Novgorod

Kiev

Normandy

Istanbul

THE VIKING WORLD

The Vikings built fantastic ships that let them sail further than any other Europeans at that time. They settled in parts of Scotland, Ireland, England, Iceland, Greenland and Normandy. Some reached Newfoundland (North America) while others sailed down the rivers of Russia to trade.

MAP KEY

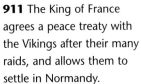

Viking homelands

Viking settlements

---

911 The King of France agrees a peace treaty with the Vikings after their many raids, and allows them to settle in Normandy.

c.980 Erik the Red discovers Greenland. After five years, Vikings from Iceland begin to settle there.

c.1000 Leif Eriksson sails from Greenland to North America. He calls the land he discovers "Vinland".

1066 William, Duke of Normandy, invades England. The Viking age soon comes to an end.

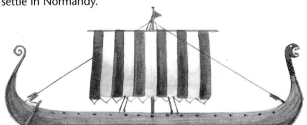

HOW DO WE KNOW ABOUT THE VIKINGS?

Many clues to life in Viking times come from evidence discovered by archaeologists. By carefully excavating artefacts and other evidence from a site and studying them, historians and archaeologists can build up a picture of how people lived in that place at a certain time in the past. The examples shown on this page give a selection of surviving objects from Viking times. There are also some standing structures, like rune stones, and written records from which we can learn.

An archaeological dig in progress at York, England. It has given us a wealth of information about Viking life.

LEATHER AND WOOD

Objects made from leather and wood usually rot but if the soil is damp, this can help preserve them. Viking shoes and wooden bowls have been found.

Viking gold coins

Viking wooden bowl

COINS

Gold and silver coins have been found on many Viking sites. By looking at where the coins were made, archaeologists can learn about where the Vikings travelled and traded.

Carved wooden panel at Urnes Church, Norway.

WOOD CARVINGS

From the few examples which have survived we know that the Vikings were skilled wood carvers. The wood carving (*left*) dates from the late 1100s, at the end of the Viking era.

Viking comb

EVIDENCE IN THE LANDSCAPE

The remains of some Viking buildings and graves can still be seen today.

A Viking grave at Ballandorae, Isle of Man.

BONES AND ANTLERS

People have found combs on Viking sites, like this one made from a deer antler. The Vikings carved many objects from bones and antlers, including ice skates, buckles and musical instruments.

SEEDS

Archaeologists try to find out which plants and animals lived at certain times in the past. To do this, they sieve samples of the soil and examine the remains of seeds, animal bones and insects under a microscope.

Magnified seeds and other objects from a Viking site.

ON THE FARM

Most Vikings were farmers. They kept animals and grew crops. Various Viking farm tools have been found, including knives and scythes (*right*), forks, axes, spades, ploughs and sickles. Many tools had wooden handles which have rotted away.

Knife

Scythe

VIKING FARMERS

Viking farmers grew enough food to feed themselves and their families. They grew grain crops in the surrounding fields, and vegetables, such as onions, cabbages and beans, in gardens close to the home.

The Vikings kept cows, sheep, goats, pigs and hens. The cows gave them leather, as well as meat and milk. Wool from the sheep was woven into cloth. Hens' feathers were used to stuff pillows and mattresses.

THE CROPS

In the north, the Vikings grew oats, barley and rye, but further south they could grow wheat, too. Crops were often attacked by pests.

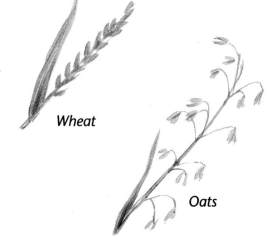

Barley

Rye

Wheat

Oats

Viking farmers harvest their crop by hand, using a sickle.

THE FARMING YEAR

In spring, the farmers ploughed the fields and sowed seeds. They spread manure on the hayfields to make the grass grow well. Animals grazed around the farm. After the grain harvest, the Vikings killed any weak animals for meat as they could not feed all of them over the long winter.

THE ANIMALS

Farm animals were smaller and thinner than they are today. Sheep and cattle had long horns.

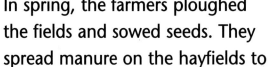

VIKING HOMES

Houses were similar across the Viking world, having just one long living room. At Stöng in Iceland (*right*), archaeologists have rebuilt a Viking home using slabs of turf – grass with the roots still attached to the soil. The original house was buried during a volcanic eruption, leaving evidence of how it used to be.

THE LONGHOUSE

Viking houses are often called longhouses because they were usually oblong in shape. The main building was up to 30 metres long and might have other buildings added on.

In the Viking homelands of Sweden, Denmark and Norway there were plenty of trees so the walls of houses were built of wood. The roofs were thatched with straw or reeds.

Vikings also built houses of wattle and daub. They wove twigs between upright posts and then "daubed" (covered) them with thick mud to keep out draughts.

BUILDING MATERIALS
The Vikings used whatever materials were available in the area. Wattle and daub, wood, turf, straw and stones were all used.

Wood

Wattle

Straw

Turf

Stones

The whole family helps out around the farmhouse. One child feeds the pigs while another scares birds off the growing crops.

DRYING FISH
Some Vikings preserved fish by drying them. They cleaned and gutted the fish and hung them over wooden racks outside.

AROUND THE HOUSE
In fine weather, the Vikings did a lot of work outside their homes. They looked after the vegetable gardens and carried out repairs to the house. Wood was chopped and stacked. Someone fetched water from a stream or well for cooking, drinking and washing. Women cleaned and treated animal skins to make leather, and hung washed clothes out to dry.

AROUND THE HEARTH

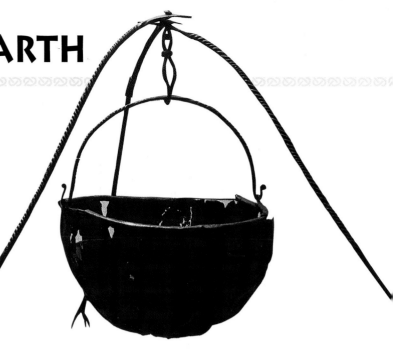

Viking homes had only one room. The hearth (fireplace) was at the centre of it. To stop the flames from the hearth spreading out, it was usually surrounded by stones or pieces of wood. An iron cauldron (*right*) hung over the fire. It was used for heating water and for cooking.

HOME LIFE

It could be quite crowded inside the house as three generations of the same family often lived together. As well as children, parents and grandparents, the family often included unmarried aunts and uncles.

Everyone lived as close to the hearth as possible. Its fire kept them warm and also gave out light, although there were lamps as well. The women prepared the food and cooked it, spun wool, wove cloth and made clothes around the hearth. Everyone else ate, talked and slept in the warm glow of the fire.

MYSTERY OBJECT

This object was found during excavations in York, England. It is made from iron and is 8.6 cm long. It has been taken apart for this photograph but when in use, it all fitted together. It helped Vikings keep their belongings safe. What do you think it is?

(Answer on page 32.)

Life inside a longhouse.
It could be smoky indoors
as often smoke did not escape
through the hole in the roof,
as it was meant to.

MAKING YARN

Wool

Comb
for fleece

Spindle

Whorl

Women made yarn (thread)
and wove it into cloth on
looms (*see picture above*).
First they combed the sheep's wool to
remove any tangles. Then they spun it into
yarn by fixing a thread from the fleece to
the spindle and setting it spinning. As it
dropped to the floor, it twisted more and
more of the wool into yarn.

FURNITURE

Viking homes did not contain much
furniture. Wealthier families might have
a wooden table but few chairs. Most
people sat on the floor or on benches
built into the walls of the house. At
night, they spread out blankets and
animal skins stored in chests and
turned the benches into beds.

EATING AND DRINKING

There were two main meals a day – one in the morning and the other in the evening. Most people ate their meals from wooden plates and drank from wooden cups. They used pottery jars (*right*) to store food, such as flour, nuts or milk. Only wealthy Vikings used pottery plates and cups as they were expensive.

THE VIKING DIET

By studying the bones and seeds found on Viking sites, archaeologists can tell what the Vikings ate. As well as meat from the pigs, sheep and cattle they kept on their farms, the Vikings hunted and ate meat from wild animals, such as boar and deer. They ate eggs from hens, geese and ducks as well as berries and nuts. Bread was made from the wheat grown in the surrounding fields. People who lived close to the sea ate fish most days.

DAIRY PRODUCE

The Vikings ate a lot of dairy produce. They drank milk, as well as buttermilk, from their cows. Buttermilk was the thin milk which was left after the cream had been removed to make butter. They also made and ate cheese, using a wooden cheese strainer.

Cheese strainer

Dairy cow

14

Viking women spent much of the day baking bread and cooking meat, fish and vegetables.

MAKING BREAD

Bread was made from rye or barley flour.

The grain was made into flour using a quern (*left*). A woman or child placed the grain between the two quern stones and then turned the top stone to grind it into flour.

Women mixed and kneaded the bread dough in wooden troughs by the fire. They shaped it into loaves and baked it on a flat stone or griddle placed over the fire.

PREPARING MEAT

Women usually cut up meat and cooked it slowly in a cauldron over the fire. Vegetables and herbs gave this stew more flavour. Meat could also be roasted on a spit over the fire, or baked in a pit filled with hot coals and covered with soil.

CLOTHES AND JEWELLERY

The Vikings mainly dressed for comfort and warmth. All Vikings liked to wear jewellery and many examples of brooches, necklaces and rings have been found. Without zips or buttons, brooches (*right*) also served to hold clothes together.

CLOTHES

Men wore tight-fitting wool trousers and a long-sleeved tunic, often down to the knees. It had an open neck fastened by a brooch with a belt tied around the waist. One Viking woman is said to have divorced her husband for showing too much bare chest under his tunic!

In Norway, Sweden and Denmark, women wore a long linen under-dress and a long linen, or wool, over-dress. In Britain, women just wore the long over-dress, or shift, with an apron to protect the dress. In cold weather, people wore wool cloaks. Children dressed in small versions of their parents' clothes.

MYSTERY OBJECT

This object was found in a woman's grave. It was found with a smooth glass object. Together they helped Vikings stay smart. Any ideas? (Answer on page 32.)

A Viking family dressed in the clothes of the day.

Both men and women wore flat leather shoes or boots, fastened around the ankle with a leather thong.

HOW DO WE KNOW?

No complete Viking outfit has been found as cloth rots quickly. However, archaeologists have found scraps of cloth and we do have written descriptions of people's appearances, as well as stone carvings. Also, by examining the small scraps of clothing, we know that wealthy Vikings loved to wear brightly coloured clothes. The dyes came from plants such as woad (blue dye), madder (red dye) and weld (yellow dye).

VIKING WARRIORS

Viking stories tell of the bravery of warriors. They were expected to follow their local lord or king into battle, or on a raid. In the early days, Vikings fought for their local leader. Later on, warriors fought for their king and were organised into armies. Warriors wore helmets *(right)*, mostly made of leather but some of iron.

THE FIGHTING LIFE

Warriors usually fought on foot in small groups and had to rely on surprise attacks to defeat their enemies. If the enemy fought back strongly, the Vikings made a defensive wall from their wooden shields and fought as a group from behind it.

Their favourite weapons were the longsword and the battle axe which could slice through helmets and heads.

WEAPONS
We know a lot about Viking weapons because many of them were buried with their owners. Swords were warriors' prized possessions and were often named. Warriors also used knives, called scramasax, in hand-to-hand fighting.

The Vikings rowed their ships right up to the shore so that warriors could wade ashore quickly.

Instead of fighting the Vikings, some French and English kings chose to pay the Vikings to leave them alone. This money was called the Danegeld.

RAIDING

When the Vikings raided a town or a monastery, they took all the treasure they could find and shared it out amongst themselves. They also captured as many people as possible to make them into slaves. Some slaves went to work for the Vikings but many more were sold in the slave markets of the Middle East. The first raids were on coastal towns but later the Vikings started sailing up rivers and attacking inland towns.

SHIPS

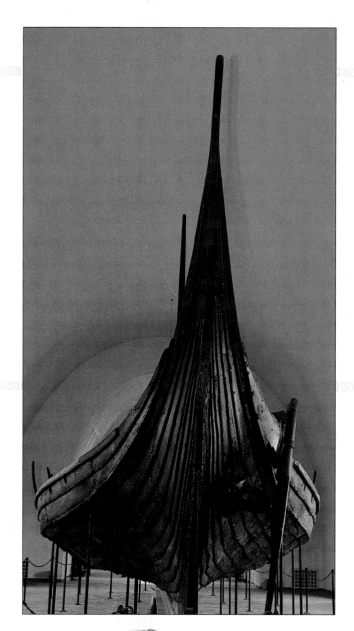

The Vikings were excellent sailors and built ships for sailing up rivers and across seas. Almost all of them have been lost except for a few which were used as burial sites for wealthy people. The ship (*right*) was discovered in 1904 under a mound of earth and was used as a burial ship for a Norwegian woman around 850.

TRAVEL BY SHIP

The best-known Viking ships are the longships which the Vikings used to go raiding and settling. They were up to 30 metres long and travelled fast, powered by their sails. If the wind dropped, they used oars. Cargo ships were shorter and wider than longships, making them slower but giving them plenty of room for goods. There were also fishing boats and small boats to carry people across rivers and lakes.

The Vikings used snowshoes to help them walk in deep snow.

*TRANSPORT ON LAND
The Vikings used wheeled carts on their farms, pulled by horses. This decorated cart was placed in a burial mound – normal carts would have been plain.*

The shape of Viking ships let them speed through the water. There was no cabin so it could be wet and cold on board ship.

VIKING ROUTES TO THE WEST
The earliest Vikings to sail west from Norway reached the Shetland and Faroe islands. Next, they reached Iceland and Greenland. In c.1000, Leif Eriksson sailed from Greenland to reach the coast of Newfoundland, now in Canada.

TRAVELLING TO NEW LANDS
Viking ships could survive rough seas because they were strong but flexible. Their design was so good that the Vikings were able to sail across the North Atlantic. A few of them even visited North America. Many more took their families and farm animals to settle in Iceland and Greenland. Away from land, the Vikings navigated by using the stars and the sun.

CRAFTS

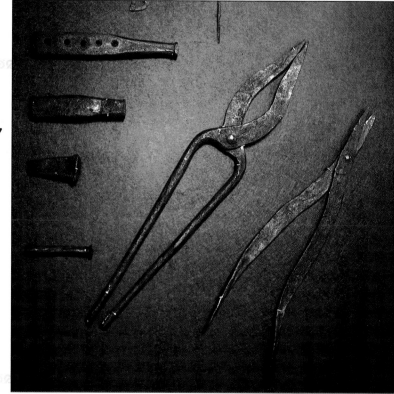

Most Vikings lived a long way from a town. Because of this, they made most of the everyday things they needed themselves. However, there were craftsmen in towns and travelling craftsmen who went from farm to farm. These tools (*right*) belonged to a Viking blacksmith. They are very similar to modern tools.

CRAFTSMEN

In Viking towns, people could buy a range of hand-crafted items. Craftsmen often sold to the public from stalls set up in front of their workshops.

Some craftsmen built ships, while others made the nails that held the planks of wood together. Many made everyday goods such as wooden cups, bowls and plates and objects made from bone or antler, like combs and buckles. Some metal-workers produced elaborate pieces of jewellery while others worked in iron to make heavy tools and locks. People who made weapons were rewarded well.

TURNING A WOODEN BOWL

The wood turner cut the wood roughly into shape and fastened it onto a pole-lathe.

Powering the lathe with his foot, the wood turner set it spinning. Then he held a chisel against the wood and hollowed the middle out as it spun.

He shaped the outside of the bowl in the same way before taking it off the lathe.

To make a sword, a blacksmith heated two rods of metal in the fire, then twisted them together. Here he is heating them again and hammering them flat to make a strong blade.

POTTERY
In England, the Vikings used pottery for jugs and storage jars, cooking pots and oil-lamps.

BONE AND ANTLER
The Vikings carved pieces of bone and antler into many objects including belt buckles, combs, game pieces and ice skates.

METAL
Metal-workers made some of the most valuable items in the Viking world – swords, axe-heads, nails for boat-making, locks, tools and jewellery.

BUYING AND SELLING

Many Vikings traded as well as farmed, travelling from farm to farm between haytime and harvest to buy and sell goods. Some Vikings exchanged goods for those of equal value. Viking merchants bought goods with coins, or with pieces of silver or jewellery, weighed on scales like these (*right*), to work out their value.

TRADERS

Most of the trading happened at markets in towns such as Birka in Sweden, Hedeby in Denmark, Kaupang in Norway, York in England and Dublin in Ireland. Traders exchanged their goods for other things of at least equal value. Then they went back home, or on to another market to sell the second lot of goods for a profit.

The Vikings sold or exchanged goods such as timber, honey, tin, iron, wheat, wool, leather, fish and walrus ivory. They bought items such as fine cloth, jewellery, glassware, pottery, spices, wine and slaves.

Some of the goods brought back from trading trips have been found in Sweden. They include glass from Germany and pottery from the Mediterranean.

Glass cup and pottery jug and cup

A Viking merchant uses his scales to pay for some precious silk cloth.

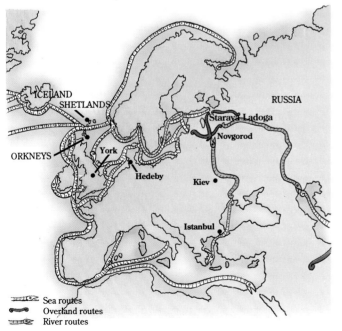

Sea routes
Overland routes
River routes

ICELAND
SHETLANDS
ORKNEYS
York
Hedeby
RUSSIA
Staraya Ladoga
Novgorod
Kiev
Istanbul

TRADE ROUTES TO THE EAST

Viking traders from Sweden crossed the Baltic Sea to sail down the Russian rivers. Some went as far as Baghdad (in modern Iraq), others to Kiev (Ukraine) and on to Istanbul (in modern Turkey). They traded with Byzantine Greeks and Arab merchants.

The main trade routes (left) took the Vikings west beyond the Arctic Circle, south into the Mediterranean and east to Russia and beyond. In places where rivers were difficult to sail, they lifted the ships out of the water and carried them overland.

VIKING RELIGION

The Vikings worshipped many gods and goddesses. Memorial stones, such as this one (*right*), can help explain some Viking beliefs. This one shows two warriors travelling to the underworld, Valhalla, in a boat. The Vikings believed that the spirits of warriors who died in battle would go to live in Valhalla, the home of Odin, their most important god.

GODS AND GODDESSES

When the Vikings settled in Britain, they continued to worship their gods. We can still read many fantastic stories they told of the battles between the gods and their enemies, the giants. The three main gods were Odin, god of wisdom and war; Thor, the protector of ordinary people; and Frey, the god of fertility and birth.

Gradually, Vikings in Britain became Christian. Some Vikings continued to worship the old gods, alongside the Christian god.

This stone mould shows that Christian beliefs existed alongside the old Viking gods. The jeweller who used this mould made Christian crosses and lucky charms in the shape of Thor's hammer.

Christian cross

Thor's hammer

The cremation of a wealthy Viking.

ODIN

ODIN
Odin was the god of kings, warriors and poets. He was the most important of all the Viking gods.

THOR
Thor was the most popular Viking god. He was big and strong and is often shown with the hammer he used to battle with the giants.

VIKING FUNERALS

Many Vikings believed that a dead person's spirit sailed to the underworld in a ship. Because of this, wealthy Vikings were cremated or buried in a ship, together with all the items they might need for their journey. Poorer Vikings set up stones in the shape of a ship around the grave of their loved one. Ordinary people went to an underworld called Hel while warriors who died in battle went to Valhalla (*see top left*).

ENTERTAINMENT

For everyday relaxation, Vikings sat around the fire listening to each other tell stories. When a wealthy Viking put on a feast, there was food, music and story-telling, sometimes by travelling poets (see page 30). The Vikings also enjoyed board games played on wooden game boards, like this one (*right*), and sports.

SPORTING COMPETITIONS

In the summer, the Vikings enjoyed sporting competitions. There were swimming and rowing races, wrestling matches and weight-lifting competitions, as well as horse races. One competition challenged contestants to walk all around the outside of a longship by stepping from oar to oar as it was being rowed.

Children played a kind of football as well as other ball games. They also had model boats, wooden swords and wooden dolls for the girls.

FEAST TIME

Written records tell us that the Vikings often wore their best clothes at feast times. They visited each other's homes and drank beer or mead from a drinking horn that was passed from drinker to drinker until it was empty.

Drinking horn

THE FEASTS

The Vikings had three main feasts, or holidays. Each feast could last two weeks and took the form of lots of eating, drinking, singing, dancing and story-telling.

Vikings enjoy the meal while their children play a game.

VIKING GAMES

Vikings who travelled to the east watched the Arabs playing chess and brought the game back home with them.

These Viking chessmen were found on the Isle of Lewis, Western Isles, Scotland.

Viking playing pieces used in Viking games were made from glass, stone, bone, wood or ivory.

WRITING AND STORY-TELLING

Many Vikings were great story-tellers but few knew how to write anything down. Those that could write used letters called runes. Runes were also carved onto memorial stones, usually called rune stones. This one (*right*) is in memory of a man called Ulf from Sweden who died around 1020. The runes are all round the edge.

STORIES

Viking families often spent the long winter evenings sitting around the fire, telling old stories and making up new ones. They learnt the stories by heart and passed them down the generations.

Many of the stories were legends, based on the adventures of the Viking gods. People liked to hear stories about the god, Thor, and his struggles with the giants. They also liked to hear about the lives of the Viking kings and adventurers. These stories, called sagas, were particularly popular in Iceland where many of the adventurers had lived. Most of the sagas were written down in the 13th century by an Icelander, Snorri Sturluson, and can still be read today.

VIKING POETRY

The Vikings enjoyed listening to poems. Wealthy people often invited a poet to their home to entertain guests. The poet read out some of his poems and made up new ones in praise of the home-owner. The payment was often a piece of jewellery, like this bracelet.

A rune-master carves a memorial stone. Rune-masters carved the stones in the field or place where the stones were going to stand as they were too heavy to move around.

f	u	th	o	r
k	h	n	i	a
s	t	b	m	l	R

RUNES

Viking runes were made up of straight lines (*see left*). This made them easier to carve. However, as there were only 16 letters, there wasn't one for every sound in the language. This made it difficult to read or write runes as many words had letters missing from them.

INDEX

ANSWERS TO MYSTERY OBJECT BOXES

Page 12: This object fits together to form a lock and key.

Page 16: This object was probably a type of ironing board. The glass object was rubbed over cloth laid on the board to smooth it.